The Work of the Cross

Taylor Kerby

WESTBOW*
PRESS
A DIVISION OF THOMAS NELSON
& ZONDERVAN

WestBow Press books may be ordered through
booksellers or by contacting:

WestBow Press
A Division of Thomas Nelson & Zondervan
1663 Liberty Drive
Bloomington, IN 47403
www.westbowpress.com
1 (866) 928-1240

ISBN: 978-1-4908-4576-0 (sc)
ISBN: 978-1-4908-4575-3 (e)

Library of Congress Control Number: 2014913404

Printed in the United States of America.

WestBow Press rev. date: 07/31/2014

Contents

Preface

At the literal crux of human history Christ hangs on a tree. Jesus' bloody death is an event that has haunted, convicted, blessed, confused, saved, or condemned everyone who has ever lived. In this book we will look at the atonement, which is the reconciliation of all things to God. This book is going to go as in depth as possible to explore the many things that were accomplished by Jesus' death on the cross. There are many Christians in the church today that hear what Christ did but do not fully grasp the power of it and why it is so great. That is the very reason this book was written. This will help us to understand all the reasons that Christ chose to die and what it has done for the entire world. Just like a jewel has many different sides that show many different beautiful things; the crucifixion also has many different beautiful works that changed the whole world. As we venture through each work, there will be scripture to back it up and historical accounts, where needed, to fully explain the point at hand. Some of the things discussed will hopefully challenge you to seek out the Bible to make sure what I am stating is true. It is not my goal to persuade you to believe everything presented but to give you the information that God has given me about what has all happened because of the cross. What you choose to do with this information is completely up to you. I just pray that you will take it and dwell on it and that through this study you may come to learn more about the Lord that gave everything just for you to be with Him. I hope you enjoy *The Work of the Cross.*

✝

CHAPTER 1

The Crucifixion of Jesus Christ

The most interesting thing about Jesus Christ's time on this earth was His crucifixion. This is where he overcame the devil and reconciled everything back to God. Before we dive into everything that Jesus accomplished through His death, I want to look and what crucifixion is and how it was for Jesus.

Crucifixion is the most horrendous, despicable, painful, and agonizing form of death. The ancient Jewish historian Josephus said that it was the most wretched of all deaths. Crucifixion has always been reserved for the most disgraceful deaths. Crucifixion is so unbearable that the word "excruciating" was created to define it. Excruciating literally means "from the cross." Crucifixion began about five hundred years before

1

the birth of Jesus. It was the Persians who invented it, but the Romans perfected it and it was reserved for the lower-classes and for slaves or foreigners. It was extremely rare for a Roman citizen to be crucified. A death by crucifixion was often slow and agonizing. The person being crucified would die by asphyxiation which means that they would die from choking because they could not push themselves up enough on the cross to get a breath. Crucifixion was always done openly and publicly. In some instances it would actually take days for a person to die. One thing that would be done on occasion to prolong death was that a ledge would be placed under the person's buttocks so that they were held up a little and this would allow them to be able to receive oxygen. Most people wanted to die as quickly as possible so they would actually push themselves off the ledge so that it would be less agonizing. In an effort to make sure that they stayed on the ledge a seven-inch spike would be nailed into the man's penis. This was the most excruciating way to die at that time and most people would never receive a decent burial.

Now I would like to discuss the last days of Jesus' life and try to describe His death so we know what He really did when he died. Approaching His death, Jesus celebrated the Passover with His disciples. The Passover was first started in the Old Testament when

Moses went to Pharaoh to ask him to let the people of Israel go. When Pharaoh denied letting them go; God sent a number of plagues on Egypt. The final plague was that any house not marked with the blood of a lamb would have the life of the firstborn son taken by the angel of death. Any house marked with the blood of the lamb was a house that the angel of death would pass over and no one would die in that house. It was the Israelites that marked their houses with the blood and all the Egyptians did not, so all firstborn sons died and afterward Pharaoh let the people of Israel go. This was a day that the Israelites celebrated every year. It was during this time that Jesus poured the wine and said, "This is my blood. Drink this in remembrance of me." He also broke the bread and said, "This is my body that was broken for you. Do this in remembrance of me." This was also the time that the Bible says that Satan entered into the heart of Judas Iscariot and he left the dinner. After this Jesus and the eleven disciples left and went to the Garden of Gethsemane, where Jesus prayed to God for any other way to bring reconciliation so that He would not have to be crucified. The Bible says that in light of the anguish Jesus was about to endure, He began to sweat blood. Doctors would say that this only happens when a person is undergoing the most extreme emotional and psychological trauma. Then

Judas Iscariot came with Roman soldiers and showed them who Jesus was by kissing Him on the cheek. He betrayed Jesus for thirty pieces of silver which fulfills the prophecy given in Zechariah 11:12-13. The soldiers arrested Him and then made Jesus walk a few miles to a place where they ran Him through a succession of false trials and false charges. They then decided to sentence Him to death. This was a breaking of all the laws. It was not a fair trial. It was not even done publicly. It was truly just murder. Then they blindfolded Jesus and had many people beat him mercilessly. They also stripped Him naked in shame and disgrace and had Him scourged. In scourging they would strip a man and shackle his hands above His head and a Roman executioner would deliver multiple blows to the body. They would whip the man with a cat of nine tails, which was a whip with nine strands of leather. At the end of each strand were metal balls and when they beat the prisoner it would tenderize their back like meat. They did this so it would be easy for the hooks of another whip to sink into the flesh. They would use the other whip and beat it into his body. They would then give a tug to make sure all the hooks had found flesh on the back and in the legs, into the skin and the bones and joints of the prisoner. The executioner would then use both hands to yank them out searing the flesh with it and even bringing out muscles, tendons, and ligaments. It would even occasionally rip a rib right out of the body. This happened over and over to Jesus to the point that the Bible records that He was unrecognizable. Then to mock Him they made a crown of thorns and shoved it many inches deep into the head of Jesus because He proclaimed that He was the King of Kings. They also put a robe around Him which served as gauze would. It seeped into the wounds on His back. His skin was just like ribbons fluttering in the wind. They let the robe remain on Jesus until it was affixed on His wounds and then they ripped it off Him. Then they handed Jesus His cross, which weighed over one hundred pounds. This was a cross that had been used before. It had nail holes and was covered with the blood of other men. They laid it on Jesus' raw, open back. It was a rugged cross with splinters that deeply penetrated what was left of His back and legs. They were making Him carry it to His place of execution and He was so tired and weak that He could not carry it on His own. They then pulled a man from the crowd named Simon and had him help Jesus carry it to the place He was going to be crucified. When He got to the place of His execution they ripped out His beard and spit on Him and mocked Him even more. They then took spikes between five and seven inches long and nailed His hands and feet to the cross. This made every breath and every movement extremely excruciating. They then dropped it into a hole and nailed above His head a sign that said, "Jesus of Nazareth, King of the Jews." This is when His breath became very heavy and much labored. At this time some who were being crucified would spit on the crowd or even urinate on them in revenge, but Jesus did not do this. He was willing to go through all of this. Then Jesus gave six statements before He died. The first was that He looked at the crowd mocking Him and said, "Father, forgive them. They do not know what they do." His second statement was to the thief that was hanging with Him at his right side who acknowledged himself as a sinner and knew that Jesus did not deserve to be there. Jesus said to Him that today he would be with Him in paradise. The thief confessed His sin to Jesus and Jesus forgave him. His next statement was to His mother saying, "John will be your son. He will love you. He is a good pastor. He'll pray for you and take good care of you." He then looked at John who was the only disciple at His death and was recorded in the gospels as the disciple that Jesus loved. Jesus looked at him and said, "Now this is your mom. You will love her like I love her." In His fifth statement Jesus quoted Psalm 22:1. He looked up and cried out, "My God, My God, why have you forsaken me." This shows that at that time God separated Himself from His son. At this moment

Jesus took on every sin in the world. He became a murderer, a pedophile, a thief, a liar, an adulterer, and an idolater. He took every single sin that anyone had ever committed on Himself. Then Jesus said his final words of triumph and victory. The Bible says that it was spoken in a loud voice. Jesus used everything left to lift Himself up and cry out at the top of His lungs, "IT IS FINISHED." At that moment Jesus died for all the sinners of the world. It was at this time that the wrath of God was satisfied because it was poured out on Jesus and all the sin was consumed. Usually a Roman soldier would break the legs of the prisoner to ensure His death but it was promised in Psalm 34:20 that none of Jesus' bones would be broken and since He was already dead the soldier took a spear and thrust it up His side and into His heart sac. The Bible says that at this time blood and water flowed out which only happens if the heart of the person had actually ruptured. Jesus was ensured to be dead. He was then buried in a tomb of a rich man named Joseph of Arimathea.

This was the bloody, painful, and excruciating death of Jesus Christ. It is also the best news told of all time because at the moment of His death all things were reconciled back to God, who created everything. Furthermore, Jesus rose from the dead three days later and after forty days of being alive again He ascended into heaven and sits at the right hand of God. Now that we know what exactly happened at Jesus' death we can begin to examine everything that was accomplished through His death.

CHAPTER 2

Jesus Died For Our Sins

Now that we have a good understanding of Jesus' death, I want to dive into the most common thing that people talk about when Jesus died. In 1 Corinthians 15:3 Paul declares to the Corinthian church that "Christ died for our sins." This is what is called the atonement; the reconciliation of all things back to God. Now one other thing that I am doing in this book besides exploring everything Christ did when He died on the cross is that I want to make all who read this into good theologians. I will do this by going into the doctrines and showing what I have found to be true by scripture. The doctrine of atonement is under attack now more than any other time in history. The problem is that many pastors shy away from the cross because it is offensive to others.

Of course it is. The Bible says that it would be. The doctrine of atonement is under attack and yet it is one of the chief accomplishments that happened at the cross.

The doctrine of Atonement begins in the Old Testament. Leviticus 16 and 17 tells us about Yom Kipper, which is translated as the Day of Atonement. The problem was that the wrath of God rested on sinful people. The Day of Atonement was a means of covering the sin that the people had committed so that they would not receive the wrath of God. On this day the High Priest would take two goats. One goat would be slaughtered. There was always blood that had to be shed to cover sin. As Hebrews 9:22 says, "Without the shedding of blood, there is no remission for sin." This also shows that the wages of sin is death. When you sin, you die. The goat dies as a substitute in our place at the hands of the High Priest. The second goat is called the "scapegoat" and it would be sent out into the wilderness. Before it would be sent out, the High Priest would lay hands on it and confess all the sins of the people and then the sin would be transferred onto that goat and it would take the sins into the wilderness. This is all a foreshadowing of Jesus. Jesus is our High Priest and all our sins were transferred to Him and His blood was shed. All the sins we have ever committed, past, present, and future were put on Him and His death causes them to be taken away from us so that we would have them no more. This is why the doctrine of atonement is so important; because without it we would still be the ones that have to die because there is nothing to take our sin away. Atonement was promised in the Old Testament, fulfilled in the life of Jesus, and echoes throughout the New Testament. This is a thread that weaves through the entire Bible. Paul writes in Romans 3:25, "God presented Jesus as a sacrifice of atonement through faith in His blood." 1 John 2:1-2 says, "My dear children, I write this to you that you may not sin. But if anyone does sin, we have one who speaks to the Father in our defense, Jesus Christ, the righteous one. He is the atoning sacrifice for our sins, and not only ours but the sins of the whole world." 1 John 4:10 says, "This is love. Not that we loved God, but that God loved us and sent His son Jesus as the atoning sacrifice for our sins." Hebrews 2:17 summarizes this entire doctrine. It says, "For this reason, He, Jesus, had to be made like His brothers in every way. In order that He might become a merciful and faithful High Priest in service to God, and that He might make atonement for the sins of His people." The theologians call this "penal substitution." This means that Jesus Christ substituted himself in our place. He was separated from the Father and the Holy Spirit and died. He did this to pay the penalty for our sin because the wage of sin is death. Jesus went to the cross as a substitute for our sin. Jesus alone can reconcile a holy God back to sinful man because He became a man and took all of the sins of the world upon Himself. Romans 5:8 says it this way, "God demonstrates His love for us in that while we were yet sinners, Christ died for us." While we were having sex out of marriage, while we were getting drunk, while we were lying, stealing, cheating, murdering, and ignoring God, He died for us. 2 Corinthians 5:21 says, "He made Him who knew no sin to be sin on our behalf, that in Him we might become the righteousness of God in Him." 1 Peter 3:18 says, "For Christ also suffered once for sins, the just for the unjust, that He might bring us to God." 1 Peter 2:24 says, "He Himself bore our sins in His body on the cross so that we might die to sin and live for righteousness. By His wounds we have been healed."

Although this is what Christ did on the cross, it would be worthless if that is how it ended. That is not how it ends though. Three days after He died, He rose from the grave. He was wrapped in one hundred pounds of burial clothing and laid in a tomb where they rolled a huge stone into the entry so no one could get in. It is a miracle that He was taken out of the burial clothes and that the stone was rolled up a hill to release Him and now He lives. The Bible at the beginning of Acts tells of how He ascended into heaven and now sits at the right hand of the throne of God. If Jesus did not rise then there would be no reason to come to God. Because He rose we can have Him come and live inside of us and when we die, if we have surrendered our life to Him, we can be with Him forever and ever. There will be no end but if you do not have Jesus then you will spend eternity in hell, which is a place of torment. If you have never surrendered your life to Jesus and want to then say this prayer and really mean everything that it says. "Jesus I know that I am a sinner. I also know that You gave your life and died on a cross to take all the sins that I have committed and will commit away. I also believe that three days later You rose again and have the victory over sin and death. I want to give you my life and have you live in me. I surrender my life to Your will. In Jesus' name, Amen." If you have prayed that prayer, you are now a member of the church and bride of Christ. Welcome. This is the greatest news to everyone in the world and it was all accomplished on the cross.

CHAPTER 3

Jesus Died to Crush Our Enemies

In this chapter we are going to look more at Christus Victor. This is the victory of Jesus over Satan, death, and demons. For this we need to see Jesus as a great warrior and king. Then we need to see Satan as a foe that stands in great opposition to Jesus. Also we need to look at our lives and the entire human history as a battleground that Jesus and Satan are fighting on. I know that right now you are probably thinking about skipping this chapter because I mentioned demons and Satan and a great battle that is going on. For some reason people get very uneasy when they start hearing that but please read on and do not skip this very important accomplishment that was made.

I want to look at a great quote by C.S. Lewis from his book *The Screwtape Letters*. "There are two equal and opposite errors into which our race can fall into about the devils. One is to disbelieve in their existence. The other is to believe and feel an excessive and an unhealthy interest in them." Basically Lewis is saying that there are two extremes, one that says there are no such thing as Satan or demons and one that focuses almost completely on Satan and demons instead of focusing enough on Jesus. We want to avoid these two extremes and try to stay on the middle ground where we believe that they are real but do not give them the focus. In the beginning the all-powerful, all knowing, great God created everything we see. He also created angels which are not all-powerful and all knowing. At one time Lucifer, who was an archangel, decided to rebel against God and he was cast out of heaven and took a third of the angels with him. I want you to understand that when we talk about a battle against God and Satan, they are not equal and that ultimately God will always win. Now we need to go to when Jesus was walking on this earth. When Jesus was alive the Bible says that He was tempted in every way that we are. Throughout His life Satan threw everything he could at Him but the Bible also says that Jesus did not sin once. Jesus triumphantly never succumbed to any temptation that Satan threw at

Him. Also while Jesus was on earth He healed many people and performed many miracles and even cast out demons. Usually what we would describe as demon-possessed today would be multiple-personality disorder. This is where there is another person that inhabits a body. This is what demon-possession truly is. What Jesus would do is talk directly to the other personality and tell it to go away and it would leave the person's body and be cast out. This happened multiple times and once a person named Legion, because he had so many demons in him, came and Jesus cast all the demons out of him and sent them to go into pigs that were near and they did. Demons had to obey what Jesus commanded them to do. Now we go to the cross and Christ is brutally beaten and hanging there almost dead and He does not look like a triumphant warrior or king. He looks like a sad, pathetic, defeated man. Even though this looks like the greatest defeat in human history it turns out to be the greatest victory. What happened is that there was a war between Satan and Jesus on the cross and Jesus triumphed over Satan and made a public spectacle of Him. He disarmed him and all his demons so that they would never be able to rule. So those of you that are scared of Satan or demons need to know that he is a defeated foe. This is a touchy subject because there are some that believe that if Satan is defeated then I should never get sick and that we are now in heaven. That is not true, you are going to get sick and I certainly hope that this is not heaven. Also there are verses that describe Satan as the prince of this world. So how can he be a prince if he is defeated? He is defeated but is not yet destroyed. He will be destroyed and then we will be with Christ in heaven forever on that day.

In the next chapter I will go a little more into how Jesus did this but what I really want to do in this chapter is show you how to defend yourself from Satan now that He has been defeated by Christ. 2 Corinthians 2:11 says, "Lest Satan should take advantage of us; for we are not ignorant of his devices." No matter what, if you know your enemy's strengths and weaknesses or his tactics and tendencies, you can defend yourself so you do not get beat up. I do not want you to get beat up but I want you to stand with Jesus as triumphant warriors. I cannot give you every tactic because it would take hours to just finish this chapter, but I will give you a brief list of some of the more common ones.

The first is simply sexual sin. In 1 Corinthians 7, Paul specifically states that sexual relationships are to be only between married couples and that if it is not, it is sin plain and simple. You might be having sex with your boyfriend or girlfriend or you are flirting outside of marriage, going to strip clubs, looking at porn, or having friends with benefits. No matter what it is, it is sin and is demonic. What Satan wants is for you to bite a hook so he can reel you in. He will bait that hook with whatever you want. He will say, "Do you want to get naked and have an orgasm? Great! Bite right here and I will give it to you." At that moment he will reel you in and you are his slave. Some people are slaves to lust and are out of control. Satan wants you to think that all sex is good. It is a lie, married sex is good and all other sex is evil.

Another common one is Christians marrying non-Christians. 2 Corinthians 6:15 basically says that marriage between a Christian and a non-Christian is like a marriage between Jesus and Satan. This will not make a happy home and you should not raise kids in that type of environment. Then there are those that say that they know a person who was dating a non-Christian and the person got saved. Great, but if they are not yet a Christian you should dump them. It's demonic. Satan loves when this happens because it weakens the witness of the Christian and ruins the legacy of the family.

One that is very common is false religions. 1 John 4 says that not all spirits are clean, good spirits. There are false teachers. Some demons will even take the name of Jesus. 2 Corinthians 11 says that there are many counterfeit Jesuses. New Age has a Jesus. Jehovah's Witness have a Jesus. Mormons have a Jesus. Everybody's got a Jesus but it is not the Jesus of the Bible. It is a demon saying that he is Jesus and hoping that no one checks. Joseph Smith, the founder of Mormonism says, "I know I have the truth because an angel told it to me." That was a demon. It says in Galatians that even if an angel from heaven preaches a different message than the gospel of Jesus they are going to hell. Mohammed, the founder of Islam, said the same thing. That an angel came to him and told him that Islam is the truth. It was a demon. The greatest lie the devil ever told is that he does not exist. He says that he is not real and that all angels are holy and good and we can trust that every single one is telling the truth. No! Some of them are demons and they want to lead you straight to hell.

Another common tactic used is bitterness. Ephesians 4 says that when we are sinned against we can either forgive or become bitter. When we become bitter we give the enemy a foothold and he will gain ground in you life. What you need to do is forgive.

Ephesians 5 talks about another tactic which is foolishness and drunkenness. The Bible says to be self-controlled and alert. When a person is drunk or gets high they are not self-controlled or alert and therefore are not able to defend themselves from the attacks of the devil.

Lastly is lying. John 8:44 says that Satan is the father of lies. Lying is his native tongue and he has been lying since the beginning.

Now you know some of the main tactics that the devil uses. I hope you remember these and do not succumb to them. If you fall into one, then it will not be hard for the devil to defeat you. But use Jesus as your strength because He has already crushed the devil. The Bible says that He is your shield and comforter. Whenever you are becoming tempted I want you to find scripture that empowers you to overcome that temptation and pray to God for the strength you need to overcome what the devil is trying to make you do. I pray that this helps you to become a conqueror and stand triumphantly with Jesus.

CHAPTER 4

Jesus Died for Our Freedom

In this chapter I am going to look at a concept that has been greatly misunderstood. It is redemption and for many years its meaning has been used wrongly which I am hoping to correct.

It started with a man named Origen, who was born in 185 A.D. Origen is the man that started teaching the doctrine of redemption and now it has become part of the Christian vocabulary. It is what I like to call Christianese. The problem is that we hear it a lot and it appears one hundred and thirty times in the Old Testament and twenty times in the New Testament but not many people truly knows what it even means. The mistake that is told by many is that it was taken from the pagan slave market. In the Roman pagan slave market redemption meant that someone outside would come in and pay a large sum of money and purchase a slave's freedom. For many years Christians have been taught that Jesus paid for us to be redeemed. Some of you reading this book have been taught that your whole life and have no idea that it was actually wrong.

There are a couple of problems with this idea. The first problem is who Jesus paid off. This has been a great debate in the church for many years. Did He pay off God or Satan? The problem is that if Jesus paid God the Father, then God is the bad guy and Jesus is the good guy. This is wrong though because they are both a part of the Trinity, which are three persons in one. The Trinity consists of God the Father, Jesus the Son, and the Holy Spirit. If that idea is true, then Jesus must also be the bad guy. See how this could never work? This would mean that there are millions of people that praise and glorify someone who truly hates them and the person that paid for their freedom also hates them. Obviously, this does not work and cannot be true. The second option is that Jesus paid off Satan. The problem with this idea is that would mean that Satan rules over Jesus and that He had to make a deal with Satan to save us. Actually if you come from a charismatic background you might have been taught that Jesus was defeated on the cross. They believe that

Jesus went down to hell and got the snot beat out of Him for three days by Satan and demons. This was to somehow pay the price and now through Jesus being defeated we are set free by Him. Not only does this idea not make any sense, but it would mean that Satan, who was a created being, has overpowered His Creator and that Jesus serves Him. That would mean that even those who follow Jesus truly serve Satan also. These are both completely wrong but are the only two options we have if Jesus paid someone off.

One more problem is that this belief comes from paganism. If this is true, then Christianity is just a modified form of paganism. Many people that go to seminary in college will be told that all Christian beliefs come from pagan ideas. This is the big thing among the new hip churches that teach a bunch of bull that is simply not true. In Leviticus 17:11 God says, "I give you this sacrifice of atonement." This is a foreshadowing of Jesus that shows it directly came from God and not some pagan belief. Paul says in Galatians 1:11-12, "The gospel that I preach did not come from human beings, didn't come from philosophers, religions, or cultures. It came from God." Redemption was revealed to us by God and He alone designed it.

Now the question is where do we go to find out what redemption truly means? The answer is that it comes from the book of Exodus. What happened in Exodus is that God's people, Israel, were in bondage to Pharaoh and he was very brutal to them and would not let them worship God. Because of this God crushed him and set His people free. There was no payment made or negotiation. God led Israel through the Red Sea and let Pharaoh get into the middle of the sea and then let it crash on top of him, which obviously killed him. That is the picture of redemption. Exodus 6:6 says, "Therefore, say to the Israelites, I am the Lord, and I will bring you out from under the yoke of the Egyptians. I will free you from being slaves to them, and I will redeem you with an outstretched arm and with mighty acts of judgment. Redemption came from Exodus when God crushed Pharaoh and set His people free.

Now if you are like me and want to find out if everything in this book is true; you might think that this is some kind of blasphemy because of some verses that say Jesus is a ransom. One verse that says this is 1 Timothy 2:5-6. Two others are Mark 10:43 and Hebrews 9:15. These all say that Jesus gave Himself as a ransom. All of you might be thinking how are you going to get out of this mess and make us believe what you have said. I cannot say that this is going to satisfy everyone, but I will give my best explanation for these verses. Whenever we sin we are breaking a commandment of

God. This makes us unable to be with God because He is perfect and our sin makes us imperfect. This means that we are basically in debt that we can't pay ourselves out of. We need to be made perfect by paying the debt that we have made through our sin. That is what Jesus did when He died. He took our sin away, which paid our debt so that if we accept Him, we can be with God when we die. Jesus paid what we could never pay on our own because it must be paid with death.

Now what shall we make of this information and how does this apply to our life? Well, we are all slaves to sin and death. As long as we have been on this earth; we have been a slave to Satan if we do not have Jesus. We do whatever we want. We are a slave. Then about two thousand years ago Jesus died on the cross and through this He defeated and crushed Satan so that anyone who accepts Him and believes in Him is set free. If you are a Christian, you are now freed from sin and death. You also have had your debt paid for and can be with God forever. That is the beauty of all this. You are set free to sin no more and even if you do, you are already forgiven because Christ crushed the one that accuses you. Walk in this freedom that has been given to you and do not become a slave any longer.

†

CHAPTER 5

Jesus Died as Our Sacrifice

Now we are going to look at a topic called "New Covenant Sacrifice." We are going to be mainly talking about blood. I am not sure about anyone else, but I kind of like bloody movies. When there is fighting like in *Gladiator* and you see blood fly because he stabbed someone. I think it is kind of cool but one thing I hate is seeing my own blood. It is one thing to see a movie with a lot of fake blood flying around, but it is a completely different thing to see it in real life. Ask any man that has watched as his children are born and he will tell you that it is literally disgusting to see all the blood and other stuff that comes out of his wife. The Bible is also a very bloody book. If you read all the way through it, you will notice many verses about death and blood. A good book to start in if you are looking for that stuff would be Judges. In Judges it talks about a fat man getting stabbed in the stomach and a woman driving a tent peg into a man's head. It is a bloody book. One thing I have noticed that is interesting is that blood is only mentioned when demonstrating a violent death or about sacrifice. Those are the only times blood is mentioned. Leviticus 17:11 states, "For the life of a creature is in the blood, and I have given it to you to make atonement for yourselves on the altar, to deal with sin." The shedding of blood is how we deal with our sin. Death is the result of sin and blood makes the atonement. The Old Testament, also known as the Old Covenant, talks repeatedly about blood as a sacrifice. The first sacrifice was made by God after Adam and Eve sinned in Genesis 3. It tells us that God covered Adam and Eve's nakedness with animal skins. There was no death before that and just like it covered their nakedness, blood covers our sin. From then on we can constantly see sacrifices to God being given and bloodshed being done. The two most famous occurrences of sacrifice are Abraham and Moses. The one with Abraham is in Genesis 22 when he is commanded by God to sacrifice his son but God stops him and provides a different sacrifice. The one with Moses is in Exodus 12. This is when God's people are held in slavery in Egypt and they were told to sacrifice a sheep and put its blood on the doorpost of their house so that during the night there would be no death to anyone in their home. God passed over those houses because of the blood. In Leviticus there are many rules about how sacrifice is supposed to be given and it demonstrates everything that is supposed to happen. The great day of bloodshed was the Day of Atonement. The Jews call this day Yom Kippur. On this day the High Priest would go into the middle of the temple and offer a sacrifice for all the people of the nation and blood would be shed. This would happen every year. One thing that you must know is that the animal used for sacrifice was always an animal that you raised and loved. It also had to be the best animal. It must have no blemish otherwise it was not valuable. There needed to be some sacrifice in giving the sacrifice. This would be like taking your most prized possession and bringing it to church and then in front of everybody we would demolish it. This would not only happen one time though, but you would constantly bring your most prized possession and you would constantly watch it be destroyed. What would also happen is that the person giving a sacrifice for his own personal sin would lay his hands on the animal and confess his sin to God. As they do this, their sin is being transferred to the animal so that it would be a substitute for them. Now some of you are probably thinking that this is animal cruelty and a terrible thing to do, but this is what our sin caused. This is what needed to happen for us to be forgiven. We should look at sin like this and see it as more than disobeying some rule but as shedding the blood of something that is innocent and beautiful so that you can walk away and not have that sin a part of your life anymore.

Now there is some problem with this old system. Psalm 51:16 says, "You do not delight in sacrifice or I would bring it. You do not take pleasure in burnt offerings." God is not happy about this at all. God created it and commanded that we do it but it is still insufficient for the sin we committed. Another thing that was wrong with this system is that many people would give a sacrifice but not love God. They would use the sacrifice to get rid of their sin but then would go sin more and then just sacrifice again to have it covered. Truly, though, their sin would never be forgiven because they did not love God.

This entire sacrificial system was to prepare us for the New Covenant system of Jesus dying for our sins. The book of Hebrews is all about how Jesus is the Old Covenant sacrifices being fulfilled through Him. In Hebrews 8:13 it says that by calling this covenant new, it makes the old one obsolete. It makes the sacrifice of animals that only last until you sin again worthless.

Basically it is saying that the Old Testament was good but it was preparing people for the New Covenant in Christ's blood. When God uses the word covenant, He is meaning relationship. For an example, when you are married, you are in a covenant relationship with your spouse. One thing that needs to happen for this to work is that you must love your spouse. If you do not love him or her then you are a hypocrite and the marriage means nothing. The same thing is true with the covenant with God. You must love Him also otherwise your sin is never truly forgiven.

Now, when you read the Old Testament, you should be able to see how it is a foreshadowing of what Jesus did for us on the cross. That is why Jesus would always win the debates with the Pharisees. They would come to Him to argue theology but He knew it was all about Himself and He corrected them every time.

Now you understand what I'm saying, but you might not fully see how Jesus' death is exactly like the Old Testament sacrifice so I will explain it a little more. Jesus Christ is the eternal God who became a man and came to us. He lived just like we live except he never sinned like we humans always do. He was unblemished and unstained. He was a perfect sacrifice. The Bible then says that He shed His blood for the remission of sins in the New Covenant which was foreshadowed by the sacrifices in the Old Testament. In fact just hours before Jesus was arrested, He celebrated the Passover with His disciples. During that meal Jesus said that the cup of wine represented His blood that was shed for our sins and that the bread represents His body that was broken for us. That is why in churches we have what is called communion. It is only done by people who have accepted Christ. Communion is when we take and eat some bread and drink wine or grape juice to remind us of Jesus and that we are in a covenant relationship with Him. If you remember in the first chapter I talked about everything that happened to Jesus and you must know that by the time He died, He was a bloody mess. There was blood all over Him and everywhere He went during that time. It is only by that blood that we are free from sin. Jesus became our High Priest and our sacrifice but instead of it only being temporary, it lasts for eternity if you have surrendered yourself to Jesus. He died to take our sins away and to be our sacrifice. He did what we could not accomplish on our own because He loves us so much. He just wants us to come to Him and live with Him in heaven forever. That is His heart. The Bible says that He will never leave you nor forsake you. The world is full of gods that hate people and are distant but the God of the Bible is full of love and always there to accept you.

Jesus is able to take all your sins away at any time. There is nothing you can do to make Him love you less or make Him not accept your sins. That is our God. That is our sacrifice.

✝

CHAPTER 6

Jesus Died for Our Unrighteousness

As I said in the beginning of this book, something that I want to make happen is to have everyone become good theologians. Everyone is already a theologian because we all have ideas about God. Even an atheist is a theologian to some degree because he has the idea that there is no God. One thing that is very sad about our world is that there are so many different opinions about God and so many people get a wrong view of the truth about Him; especially Christians. There are so many denominations and whether a person is Calvinist or Arminianist, we sometimes don't know what we truly believe. I personally just call myself a Christian. That is what I am and I had to learn not to label myself because as Christians we are to be the body of Christ and not the body of the Charismatic, or the Lutherans, or the Baptist. I want to add all this just to make sure you understand where we are going and that all I am trying to do is have you know the truth that I have found in Scripture. Also we will begin to go deeper into some theological stuff and I do not want you to get lost so make sure you are awake so I can continue without leaving anyone behind.

In this chapter we are going to talk about our unrighteousness. A lot of people may say that they know they are not perfect but they are still pretty righteous. They are wrong. Then some people will say that they know they are terrible and there is no way they can ever be right for God. They are also wrong. The truth is that we are all terrible and there is only one way that we can be right for God. That is what we will discuss now.

In Job 9:2 Job asks one of the most penetrating questions. He asks God, "How can someone who is unrighteous stand before you, the Righteous God?" The first thing you must understand is that God is righteous. Psalm 11:7, Daniel 9:14, Isaiah 45: 21, and numerous other verses all declare that God is completely righteous and cannot do anything that is wrong. If you want, you can look up those verses and see for yourself (which is what I hope you are doing with everything I say). The second issue that we must know is that we were made in

His image and likeness. Genesis 1 and 2 demonstrates the creation of everything and says that God chose to make the first humans, Adam and Eve, in his likeness and that it was very good. So this means that God is righteous and that at the beginning we were made to be righteous like He is. Now we look at the world and see all kinds of unrighteous acts. From things such as lying to things like murder and sex-trafficking. Where in the world did everything go wrong? Well Genesis 3 tells us that Adam and Eve sinned by eating the fruit that they were specifically told not to eat by God. One thing to know is that God cannot in any way do something wrong because it is not in His nature but He allowed Adam and Eve to choose to continue in their righteousness or become unrighteous. Because they sinned, unrighteousness is now a part of our nature. That means that everyone will sin and there is no way to be righteous on our own. Even a baby that is one day old is unrighteous just because of the first sin, even though that baby has not sinned yet. All we have to do to be sinful is be conceived. That is the one magic thing that must happen to make someone sinful. Psalm 51:5 says, "We're sinful from our mother's womb." Some might say that this is completely unfair. Why should one decision by a man that lived thousands of years ago make me a sinner? The reason is that Adam was the head of all of us because he was the first man and when he voted that we rebel and sin against God, it affected all of us and made us rebel against God. For example, the president of the United States decides that we need to go to war. He is not going to have everyone that lives in the nation vote on whether we should or not. He simply declares war and then we go and do it. The same thing happened here, Adam simply sinned and therefore we do it. Some of you really try to do all the right things but the truth is that in your heart you are a sinner and a lawbreaker. Nothing you do will ever make you any better. I am stressing this point to you because everyone has been lied to and some have come to believe that we can choose not to do bad things and if we just control ourselves enough, then we will be considered a good person. The problem with this is that you are saying God is a liar because He says that we are all sinners but God cannot do anything wrong. This means that He cannot lie so if you say He is a liar then you are falsely accusing God which makes you a liar and makes you a sinful person. There is no way to get around it. You are sinful and because of that you are eternally damned to hell.

Everyone deep down knows that they were meant to be righteous and we know that we are truly not, so we try to make ourselves righteous on our own. This is called self-righteousness and there are two ways that people try to do this. The first way is by morality. Romans 10:3 says, "Since they do not know the righteousness that comes from God, and sought to establish their own, they did not submit to God's righteousness." This is morality. Most of you believe that all you need to be is a very moral person and God will accept you. Truly you could be the best moral person in the entire world and sin once and be cast into hell. The main problem with morality is that if you finally achieve it then you will point your finger at everyone else. This will make you prideful which is a sin and it is what made Satan be cast out of heaven. God hates pride and that is all that morality will lead to so that is a dead end to being accepted by God. The other way people try to become righteous is by religion. They go to church and act and say all the religious things and think that they will be saved because of that. The truth is that God hates religion. Now you are saying who the heck is this man that says he is a Christian but says that he is not religious? I am a man that knows what religion really is. Religion is people trying to please God, and make themselves look good. That is all religion is and it has nothing to do with God and that is why He hates it. Jesus talks many times about the religious guys. In his day they were the Pharisees. They were the most religious and moral people that probably ever lived. They would walk around staring straight at the ground just so they would not have the chance to look at a beautiful woman. Just try for one day to stare at the ground the entire day not looking up for fear of seeing a beautiful woman. I can tell you that you will definitely bang your head a few times and that is what the Pharisees did every day. They were like this with everything, even with tithing. They would be the people that would count their toothpicks and take a tenth of them to the temple to give to God. That is pretty crazy but it is what they did. Looking at them most people would say that if anyone is able to get into heaven it would be them. The shocking thing is that Jesus uses them as an illustration. In Matthew 5:20 Jesus says, "For I tell you that unless your righteousness surpasses that of the Pharisees and teachers of the law, you will not enter the kingdom of heaven." Basically Jesus is talking to all the drunks and prostitutes and says they have to be better than Billy Graham and Mother Teresa to get into heaven. Not saying that Billy Graham or Mother Teresa are self-righteous. This is not good news. Actually this is the worst news ever. For someone to tell us that we must be better than Billy Graham to get into heaven because He is going to hell leaves us with no hope. That is what Jesus wanted us to realize. He wants us to know that the best religion and morality won't save us. Before I tell how we can be righteous I want to give you an illustration of this. Right now as I am writing this, it is four days until Halloween and I know some people are going to have candy ready to hand out. Imagine that when one of the trick-or-treaters comes to your house, instead of giving them candy, you give them a bloody tampon. Think about that for a second. THAT IS GROSS! This is biblical. Isaiah 64:6 says, "All of us have become like one who is unclean." This is like a woman on her cycle. I am hoping half of the people reading this are men because they fully know how disgusting this is. This is what happens though when we fill our buckets with all these good deeds thinking that it will save us. When you stand before God, all you will have in your bucket is a bunch of bloody tampons. I know you wish that you could wash your mental eyes right now but I need you to see how serious this problem with sin is. There is no way that we can make ourselves righteous. All we have done is make ourselves unrighteous so we need someone else to make us righteous. This is where Jesus comes in.

When God saw how we are in such a helpless state He had pity on us and set up the entire plan of redemption to make us righteous again. Everything that was lost in Adam was going to be recaptured in Jesus. God sends

His son Jesus to be born and live a perfect, sinless life. He ultimately goes to the cross and dies and that is when the most miraculous thing happens. 1 Peter 2:24 says, "He Himself bore our sins and His body on the cross so that we might die to sin and live for righteousness." This means that Jesus exchanged His righteousness for our sins and then died to forever destroy our sins so that we can be forever righteous. When He died He gave us the righteousness that we were created to have in the beginning. 1 Peter 3:18 says, "For Christ died for sins, once for all, the righteous for the unrighteous, to bring you to God." We are all unrighteous but Jesus exchanges our unrighteousness for His righteousness so that we can be righteous. All we need to do to have it is surrender our life to Him. It is not about us finding ways to get our own righteousness. It is all about Jesus giving it to us. That is the only way that we can come to God and not be holding a bucket full of bloody tampons.

CHAPTER 7

Jesus Died for Our Justification

In this chapter we will discuss justification by faith and these are big words and massive theology so I hope that you will be able to keep up. This has been one of the most conflicting issues in the Christian faith. There have been arguments about it for the past two thousand years and I hope to clarify it in this chapter. First, we must start with a right view of God. We must understand that God is good, holy, righteous, and just. We need to see Him as the King on His throne and as the judge looking down at everyone's life and everyone's heart. God deals with us by the law and for us to fully understand justification we must look at everything from His angle. We cannot look at this from our angle because we are sinners and will try to justify ourselves which is what I do not want us to do. We also must understand the law. Many people, even some reading this book, hate the law and deliberately break it just to show that they are above it. Their law truly is to break the law, so they are still under a law, but that is a completely different topic. The reason that we have a law at all is so people that are weak or don't have power can get justice. The law cannot show favoritism and gives justice to all that deserve it. The problem is that the law is implemented by sinners in this world so it does not always work perfectly. There are times that injustice happens and there is no way for it not to happen. When we look at this with God using the law though, we see that there is no way there can be injustice. Because God is perfect and knows the thoughts and intents of every heart, there would be no way for Him to give wrong punishment. God judges us by what is called the Torah. It is a word that appears over two hundred times in the Old Testament. The Torah is just simply the first five books of the Bible. It is Genesis, Exodus, Leviticus, Numbers, and Deuteronomy. This is known as the law that was given by God and God still judges every human being by it. The Scripture is the first place that we have the law; but for everyone in the whole world to be judged by it, there must be some way that everyone can know it.

There is one other way that we know the law and that is what is known as the conscience. Our conscience is our spirit speaking to us telling our mind what is right and what is wrong. For instance, whenever you tell a lie you usually have a scared feeling that the person you are lying to might find out the truth. That is part of your conscience. When you steal something you always hope that no one finds out and you try to cover it up because your conscience tells you that it was wrong. This enables everyone to be able to know what is right and wrong so that we can all be judged equally. We will all some day be judged by God. What He will do is take the law that He put in our heart and the law that is written in Scripture and see if our life matches up. Sadly, we know already that our life would not match up perfectly. You might say it doesn't match perfectly but I am still a good person and don't do anything too bad. I should not be punished. Punishment is only for the people who rape and kill others. It is not for me. God does not see it this way. God sees that you in some way disobeyed the law because He is perfect and just. He does not see it in degrees. He only sees it as just or unjust, righteous or unrighteous. There is no bell curve and we are all sinners so He must deliver some type of punishment. He gives the same punishment to everyone. That punishment is spending eternity in Hell.

Anyone who breaks any part of the law of God will be judged as guilty and be cast into Hell for all eternity. You need to understand that if you break any part of the law then you will receive the punishment of being cast into Hell. We also must know that God does not just judge our actions but He judges our heart. He sees the motives of the things we do. Many times people can do good things with bad motives. One scenario that happens many times is when men go to great lengths for women, hoping that they will sleep with them. That is a bad motive. Also we can do things so that people will think that we are a good person and will believe that we are great Christians who don't do horrible things. That is a terrible motive because it is not true and when a person falls from being on that type of pillar, they will crush everyone under them. Just imagine going through your life with a teleprompter on your head showing all of your motives. It would be terrible if we have all these motives to show. That is how God sees us though. He sees all of our motives and will judge whether they are good or bad. The same thing happens here. We are either perfect and go to heaven or we fail once and are cast into Hell. This makes it certain that there is no way to get to heaven because we have all failed at least once in one of these areas. Because of our failures, we are made enemies of God. What happens when we sin is that we are dead to God and alive to Satan. We cannot be alive to God if we have sin in our lives. Now that we have examined all of this, the question we should ask is; how could a just God look at our lives with the just law and not cast us into Hell?" Exodus 23:7 says that God will not acquit the guilty. In Proverbs 17:15 God says, "Acquitting the guilty and condemning the innocent; the Lord detests them both." Also if God looked at us and acquitted us, then He would not be a just God and we would not want to follow Him or have any respect for Him. This would be like a person that is on trial for murder and he pleads guilty and the judge sets him completely free. There is no justice in that and yet it would be like God not casting us into hell. The truth is that God always gives the right verdict and the verdict that He gives all of us is that we are sinners and are condemned. How then can we get to Heaven? You should know by now that the answer is always Jesus. It is all about Jesus and His death on the cross. Jesus is completely just and takes all our sin on Himself and gives us His righteousness. That is the doctrine of justification. That is the work of the cross.

This is where a lot of debate comes in mostly between Catholics and Protestants. I do not want you to think that I hate Catholics and only love Protestants. Truly I just want you to know truth. I told you earlier that I have decided not to label myself but I will discuss subjects of debate to make sure you know truth. The Catholics believe that all the saints have extra righteousness and that if you pray to them, they will give you some of their extra righteousness that they apparently don't need. Most Catholics do not pray to Jesus but only to His mother Mary. They believe that there is a gap between us and Jesus and because Jesus is a good boy, He will do whatever His mother asks Him. For this reason they pray to Mary so that she can ask Jesus to do things for them. This is part of why they believe that justification through faith is wrong and that if a person believes it then they are going to Hell. They do not believe that anyone can go to Jesus and be saved through Him. To better understand this we need to start at the beginning.

It all kicked off in the days of Martin Luther. At this time the Catholic Church would say that you are saved by baptism. They believe that you are saved through being baptized in the church. There are two problems with this idea. The first is that it leaves Jesus completely out of the salvation of a person. The second is that baptism is just simply a public display for showing that a person has chosen to follow Jesus and has died to their sin. It has nothing to do with their salvation except to let other people know that they are now a part of the family of God. In the Catholic Church a person will get baptized as a baby, before they can truly make the decision to follow Jesus. Then when they sin in their life they must go to the priest to be forgiven. They believe that the mediator between God and man is the priest and not Jesus. The priest would forgive the person and then give them a penance. The penance was the way to work off your sin. The priest would say that you need to pray this many times and do this many good deeds and then God would wash you free from all your sin. That was how you were to be forgiven in the Catholic Church. Then if you commit a really bad sin, you would lose your salvation and go to Hell. If it was just not that bad of a sin, then you would be sent to purgatory. Purgatory is like prison. A person goes there for a certain amount of time to pay God off for their sin. I am not saying that all Catholics believe this but many do and this is why there is such a great debate. People believed all of this until a man named Martin Luther came along. He was a Catholic monk but said that through the reading of the Bible it didn't seem that people were justified by baptism, penance, confession, or any of the other things that were greatly believed at that time. He said that the Bible pretty clearly explains that a person was saved by Jesus Christ alone. This is when the Protestant Reformation came and the Catholics and Protestants split over this issue called justification by faith. That is the truth though. We are saved by grace through our faith in Jesus Christ. The reason I talk about this is because I do not want anyone to believe that they can be forgiven by baptism, penance, or anything else besides our faith in Jesus Christ. If you believe that you can get salvation any other way then you will try to get it some other way but you will go to Hell. I know this sounds harsh but it is the truth. I do not want anyone to go to Hell and that is the very reason I take this so seriously. We need to understand how we are justified otherwise there is no way that we can be saved.

Now I want to give you some Scripture that states this doctrine of justification by faith. First we are justified by grace which is told in Titus 3:7. Romans 5:16-17 says that the gift (justification) followed many trespasses because of God's grace. The second point is that it is through faith in Christ alone. Romans 4:3-5 says that Abraham believed God, which means He had faith in God, and it was credited to Him as righteousness. Abraham was not righteous but the Bible says that righteousness was given to Him by his faith in God. You see we are unrighteous but Jesus takes our unrighteousness on the cross and gives us His righteousness by our faith in Him. We do not deserve it but God loves us so much that He makes it available in this way to us. We are saved by grace alone, through faith alone, in Jesus Christ alone. That is the doctrine of justification by faith and that is the only way our sins can be forgiven.

✝

CHAPTER 8

Jesus Took Our Wrath

In this chapter I am going to push you. Some of you could get very mad and want to throw the book away (if you haven't already) but I want you to just hang in there and if you hate this chapter then just simply disregard it. I need to tell you that you have probably been lied to at least sometime in your life about God. You have been told that God is loving, gracious, merciful, kind, compassionate, and is some sort of fairy that has a big bucket of lollipops for everyone because we are such good people. That is not entirely true. Unfortunately, what many people and churches do is pick all the verses on God's love and mercy and only give sermons on those. By doing this they are not presenting all of the Scripture and we will ultimately get the wrong view of God. In the Bible God is more commonly referred to as being angry, hateful, and wrathful. If we had the mountain of verses that are about God's love next to the mountain of verses about His wrath; the wrath would be much larger. We like to ignore that and in Romans 1 it says that we suppress the truth and the unrighteousness of our deeds. So instead we have made God how we wish He would be. Because of this we have made a God that is a lot like us. In this chapter I want to set aside all the verses that you know and love and focus on the ones that you most likely hate. We have been told many times that Jesus loves me but never told Jesus hates me. I want to look at this other side and as it is said in Proverbs, "The fear of the Lord is the beginning of wisdom." So I hope you really try to follow me through this even though it might go to a place you do not really want to go.

The primary attribute of God is not His love. It is the holiness of God. His holiness is mentioned more frequently and means that He is sinless, perfect, and good. The problem with us is that we are unholy. Romans 6:23 says, "We all have sinned and fall short of the glory of God. In 1 John 1 it says that if we say we are not sinners then we are liars because God says we are sinners and He is right. Isaiah 53 says we have all sinned and gone our own way. I know you are tired of me telling you this but you are a sinner. A holy God and an unholy people would not make a good relationship. The Bible would say that we are unequally yoked. Unequally yoked means that you are not compatible and could truly never have a good loving relationship when it all comes down to it. We do not usually see this as a problem because we are sinners and would love to hang out with God. The problem is that God sees us as sinners and does not want to be around us. Genesis 6:5-6 says, "The Lord saw how great man's wickedness on the earth had become and that the inclination of every thought of his heart was only evil all the time. The Lord was grieved that He made man on the earth, and His heart was filled with pain." This is six chapters into human history and God sees that we are all completely evil and is sad that He even created us. You have been told that you are His favorite creation and right here it says that He would have rather not even created you. He would choose a spider or snake over you right now. When God sees us He is grieved and not filled with joy and gladness. Isaiah 52:9 says, "Your iniquities have separated you from God and your sins have hidden His face from you." God cannot even look at us because He is so disgusted with what we have become. I will give you a humorous example of the relationship we have with God. If you have been to Florida you have probably seen couples where the woman is walking in front and looks fine but the man is walking eight feet behind her. Not only that but he is hunched over and vibrating and murmuring all these things to himself; telling himself that he is a man and he is the head of the family and that she can no longer tell him what to do. If you have seen it you know exactly what I am talking about and it is pretty funny and sad to see people like that. This is our relationship with God though. He is like the woman and is completely fine and we are like the man hunched over telling ourselves that we are good and are loved by God and that He will let us into heaven because of His love. Psalm 5:4 says, "You are not a God who takes pleasure in evil; with the wicked you cannot dwell." God would never pick you to come and be with Him. He is disgusted with you and hates you because all you are is an evildoer and a sinner.

The next attribute I want you to look at is God's anger. Many Christians have a hard time believing that God gets angry but it is shown throughout the Bible. He floods the earth. He sends down fire out of heaven to consume people. He kills Christians in the New Testament while taking communion (I Corinthians 11:26-30). He can get very angry. Some will then say, "How can a loving God also be an angry God?" The answer is simply, "How can a loving God not be angry?" If you truly love someone, you absolutely hate it and become angry when they do something evil. God is angry when He sees those that He loves defile and destroy themselves. That is true love. It would be like you walking in on your wife or husband having sex with another person. You would be angry. You are angry because you love her and cannot believe that she would do this to you. We do this to God countless times a day. He basically watches us have sex with someone else everyday when He wants to have a relationship with us. God's anger and love are in unison. They are not and cannot be separated. People can love a person they are angry at. That is one thing that we will all learn when we are married someday. In the same way, God loves us but is angry because of our sin. Leviticus 26:27-30 says, "In spite of this, you still do not listen to me, but continue to be hostile toward me then in my anger I will be hostile toward you. I myself will punish you for your sins seven times over. You will eat the flesh of your sons and the flesh of your daughters. I will destroy your high places, your false religions, your incense altars, and pile your dead bodies in lifeless forms of your idols. I will abhor you." God gets angry. God sees us and tells us that we better stop doing whatever the heck we want because there will be a consequence. We look at this and say that it is so wrong of God to get angry in that way and yet we get angry all the time and make ourselves justified in that anger. If you are unable to be angry, then you do not understand sin. You hear about someone murdering a child or raping someone, you should get angry. You will not say that it is fine for that person to do it. That is insanity. We get angry when others sin and yet we try to justify ourselves when we sin and do not see how angry God is. Numbers 11:1 says, "Now the people complained about their hardships in the hearing of the Lord, and when He heard them His anger was aroused. The fire of the Lord burned among them and consumed some on the outskirts of the camp." Deuteronomy 29:24 says, "All the nations will ask, 'Why has the Lord done this to this land? Why is there desolation and destruction? Why this fierce, burning anger?" God's anger is referred to as burning and smoldering throughout Scripture. Some of you will say that this is just all Old Testament. We like to think that there is the God of the Old Testament and Jesus. We think that the God of the Old Testament is mean and Jesus is this super nice guy. It's like the Old Testament was when God was a teenager and emotional about everything and when Jesus finally came is when God matured more. Actually, the God of the Old Testament is the same God of the New Testament. Jesus is also the God of the Old Testament. Jesus got angry. He threw over tables and chased people out of the temple with a whip. That is anger. Mark 3:5 says, "Jesus looked at them in anger and was deeply distressed at their stubborn hearts." One of the reasons Jesus was killed was because of His anger. We need to have the right understanding that Jesus was not just some person that went around loving everybody and singing songs about how God loves us all. We need to understand that He got angry. We also need to have a right understanding of anger. We usually see anger as a person that has a short fuse and is very quick tempered. God's anger is a perfect anger. In Exodus 34 it says that God is slow to anger. Deuteronomy 13:17 says that sometimes God turns away His anger. Isaiah 48:9 says that God's anger is sometimes delayed. We rush to judgment and violence a lot of times but God is not like that. God is patient. It says in Psalm 78:38 that sometimes God's anger is held back. God does get angry at sin but His anger is perfect. God is not only angry about sin but He hates it. If God hates sin then we need to hate sin. This is a big problem because we have been told many times to love ourselves for the way we are. We are sinners and yet we have been told even in sermons to love ourselves the way we are. We need to hate our sin. It is the reason you are separated from God. Many times though, we hate the sin in others but not in ourselves. We excuse our own sin and point the finger at everyone else. It is hard to acknowledge our own sin when we realize that we are to hate it. I always have a hard time looking at my sin the way God does but I know He hates it and I am supposed to hate it too. Proverbs 6:16-19 lists six things that the Lord hates and one that is detestable to Him. The first is haughty eyes. God hates high self-esteem. Many of you have been told that you should have a high self-esteem. God hates it. That is the same thing that got Satan cast out of heaven. The second is a lying tongue. If you are one of the people that believes you need to have high self-esteem then you also belong in this category. Third are hands that shed innocent blood. This is better explained as murder. Fourth is a heart that devises wicked schemes. Fifth are feet that are swift in running to evil things. Sixth is a false witness who speaks lies. The last one and the one that God hates the most is one who stirs up dissention among his brothers. God hates all of this. Zechariah 8:1 says, "Do not plot evil against your neighbor and do not swear falsely. I hate all this declares the Lord." God is angry and hates you because He hates sin and sin is in you. This needs to sink in because you have been told your whole life that you are so good and adorable when God is saying I hate you and you are disgusting. No one says that they love rapists but hate rape. It is the same with God. I am not saying that our hatred is right like God's is but you get the point. Many people believe that Christianity is a made up religion but nobody would make this up. No one would ever come up with a belief where God hates everyone.

Not only does God hate people but He also pours His wrath on them individually. Most theologians say that God's love is personal but that His wrath isn't. This would mean that He pours out His wrath on whoever is there. That is not true. God pours out His wrath on those that deserve it. The entire reason I am saying all of this is so that you know the real God and so that you can fully understand what He saved you from. If you have not surrendered your life to Jesus then you are not saved. God can only accept those that fully submit their lives to Him. If you do not surrender your life then you will experience the wrath of God either when you die or when He comes back. He is coming back and He is going to give everyone what they truly deserve. You can either have surrendered and be made like Christ without sin, or still have sin in your life and be cast into Hell for eternity. There is a great misconception that the devil created and is the ruler of Hell but that is not true. Hell is a place reserved for those that will receive God's wrath and He is the ruler over it. This is the God of the universe. He hates you. He loves you. He gives you the chance to be saved from His wrath but will still pour it out on those that do not submit to Him.

The Scriptures declare that God does express His wrath. Psalm 7:11 says, "God is a righteous judge, a God who expresses His wrath everyday." Exodus 22:22-24 says, "Do not take advantage of a widow or an orphan. If you do and they cry out to me, I will certainly hear their cry. My anger will be aroused and I will kill you with a sword. Your wives will become widows and your children will become fatherless." Ezekiel 16:38 says, "I will sentence to you the punishment of women who commit adultery and who shed blood. I will bring upon you the blood vengeance of my wrath and my jealous anger." Notice that the second Scripture is about men that take advantage of those that are usually desperate. The third Scripture is about women that go and seduce men. Gender does not matter when it comes to the wrath or love of God. He will punish both equally. I will also give you some verses from the New Testament. Ephesians 5:6: "Let no man deceive you with empty words for because of those things God's wrath comes on those who are disobedient." Colossians 3:6: Put to death, therefore, whatever belongs to your earthly nature: sexual immorality, impurity, lust, evil desire, and greed, which is idolatry. Because of these the wrath of God is coming." The wrath of God is mentioned throughout all Scripture and it will be poured out. There is no way to escape it unless you are holy and clean as God is. This is where God's love comes in. He sees and knows that we are hopeless. God sent Jesus to die and make justification, which is what I talked about in the last chapter. On the cross God poured out His wrath on Jesus, who is Himself. Jesus cried out and asked, "God, why have you forsaken me?" Jesus was separated from God at that time to take our wrath and punishment so that we would not suffer it. By Him being separated we can never be separated. Romans 5:9 says it this way, "Since we have been justified by His blood how much more shall we be saved from God's wrath through Him." We have been justified and made clean and holy before God. He cannot punish the righteous with the wicked. Instead He saves the righteous and pours His wrath on the wicked. This is the doctrine of propitiation. 1 John 2:2 says, "He is the propitiation for our sins, and not only for ours, but for the sins of the whole world." This is what makes us able to have a relationship with God. It is only through His love and the death of Christ that we are made righteous. Our deeds will only give us His wrath but His grace will give us His presence.

CHAPTER 9

Jesus Died as Our Example

Now we are going to look at the topic, Christus Exemplar. This means Christ as our example. In this life we need a hero or someone that we can look up to and try to imitate. We need an example. We need someone to follow. That person should only be Jesus. As Christians we are called to live our life like Jesus. One of the problems of trying to live like Christ is that we have the phrase "What would Jesus do?" It is easy to say and believe that if we just do what Jesus did then we will be all happy and nothing will go wrong. The problem is that we don't see Jesus as identifying with us when we are suffering. Does Jesus have anything for us when we are in the middle of pain, suffering and loss? How are we to be like Jesus in those times?

Can Jesus identify with us when we are going through the hardest times in our lives? The answer is yes, but there are terrible portraits of Jesus that many people have been given. The main reason we do not think that Jesus can truly identify with us when we are suffering, is in the nature of Jesus. Jesus possessed two natures which are God and human being. He was fully both in every way. The reason we don't relate to Jesus is that we do not have the divine aspect. Because of this there is no way that we can identify fully with Jesus, but can Jesus identify with us? We will come to the answer of this great question as we weave through the three misconceptions that come up regarding Jesus' two natures.

The first misconception is a non-Christian position and is normally taught by other religions. It is the belief that Jesus was a good moral example and a great teacher but that is all. He wasn't God, but was a great person and inspiration to us all. Like most heresies, this is half true. Jesus was a great person and has much to teach us, but was also God. The most famous person that held this misconception was Mahatma Gandhi. He was a Hindu teacher and said that Jesus' death on the cross was a great example to the world. He did not believe that His death really accomplished any objective. He believed Jesus was not God and He could not forgive sin, but was a great man and that we can learn a lot of principles from His life.

The modified version of this belief is known as liberal Christianity. Liberal Christianity states that we are not sinners and that sin is not our problem. We are essentially good people with hearts directed toward God and we just lack motivation. Because we lack motivation Jesus came down and lived a wonderful life and died in a noble way to have ourselves love God more with our good hearts. There are many churches that teach this and many people hold this position. This is a terrible position because it denies the reality of sin, and denies that Jesus is God dealing with our sin. It has a very low view of Scripture which then gives a very low view of Jesus because all of Scripture is about Jesus.

The third error about the two natures of Jesus is actually most commonly held by Christians. What we do many times is give an overemphasis on the divinity of Jesus. The problem is we end up saying that Hebrews 4:15 is not true. It says, "We do not have a high priest who cannot sympathize with our weaknesses, having been tempted in every way we are, yet without sin." We do not take that to mean that Jesus was ever weak or suffered. We focus so much on the divine aspect of God that when it says He was tempted we believe that He wasn't really tempted because God cannot be tempted. Also, He didn't really suffer; it just says that if He was truly a human He would be suffering. If this is true then there is no way that Jesus can relate to us since we suffer and are tempted. Many of us have the portrait of Jesus as Superman. We see Superman as Kent Clark, a mild-mannered reporter but underneath He is the Man of Steel. This is the portrait of Jesus that is most commonly given. He never suffers or gets hurt and bullets fly off of him but he disguises himself as Kent Clark. Jesus disguises Himself as a marginalized, Galilean peasant, but underneath there is a big red "S" on His chest. When Judas betrays Him and Peter denies Him it didn't hurt His feelings. When He was in the Garden of Gethsemane and He was sweating drops of blood, He was not really suffering because He is Superman. He just gives us the impression that He was suffering. When He was beaten, scourged, publically humiliated, stripped naked, and mocked, it did not really affect Him. When He was on the cross and had nails hammered through His wrists and legs He really didn't feel that because He was the man of steel. This leads to discouragement because if this is true, then there is no way for Jesus to relate to us when we are having a terrible day, so He is truly of no help. The Bible says the opposite. It says that He can sympathize with us because He has suffered and has been tempted in the same ways we have. So now the question is; how do we hold Christ as our example and still see Him as fully God? How do we have a human Jesus and still worship Him and acknowledge Him as God without believing one of these three misconceptions? To do this there are three truths that you must hold tightly in your theological system.

The first truth is that Jesus was and is eternally God. There is one God and Jesus is the second member of the Trinity. Jesus stated that He was God repeatedly throughout His life. It was one of the reasons He was killed because they said it was blasphemy. The Gospel of John was in a way written to prove that Jesus was God. In John 10:33 the Jews said, "We are not stoning you for any of these but for blasphemy because you, a mere man, claim to be God." Jesus kept saying that He was God so we need to accept and acknowledge Him as being God. The second part of the Trinity came down as the man Jesus Christ. This is called the doctrine of the incarnation. This is what we celebrate at Christmas, that God came to be with us. Romans 8:3 says, "For what the law was powerless to do in that it was weakened by the sinful nature, God did by sending His own Son in the likeness of sinful man." Also the letter of 1 John was written in large part to prove that Jesus was a man here on earth. He had a physical body and lived a physical life. The first two truths we must believe are that Jesus Christ was fully God and fully man.

Then how did Jesus live a perfect sinless life as the Scriptures teach? If He is to be our example, then we need to know how He lived His life. I know that some will be able to see the humanity of Christ but most people will begin to lean back into the divinity of Christ. He healed people and never sinned because He is Superman. The last truth we need to believe is that when Jesus was on earth, He never leaned into His divinity. He never worked out of His divinity. He really did suffer and was tempted. He always lived out of His humanity. This does not mean that He ceased being God. He just didn't avail Himself to His divinity. This is the doctrine of Kenosis and it is proven in Philippians 2:5-11. It says, "Your attitude should be the same as that of Jesus Christ, who, being in very nature God, yet He did not consider equality with God as something to be grasped taking the very nature of a servant being made in human likeness. And being found in the nature of a man, He humbled Himself and became obedient to death, even death on a cross. Therefore God exalted Him to the highest place and gave Him the name above every other name; that at the name of Jesus every knee should bow in heaven, on the earth, and under the earth, and every tongue shall confess that Jesus Christ is Lord, to the glory of God the Father." That is why Jesus' name is so important. No one cares if you say God, but if you say Jesus there is a fight on because that is the name of the one true God. Jesus came down and laid aside all His rights of divinity, lived fully out of His humanity to identify with us, and then died for us. Now He is exalted and that is the only name at which salvation is given. This should be very encouraging because we have no divinity to lean into. We are forced to not be able to lean into divinity and Jesus chose to not lean into His divinity so He lived a life just like ours.

Some of you will struggle with this because you have been taught poorly. You have been taught that we know Jesus is God because He shows the attributes of God. The only problem is that it does not line up with Scripture. Jesus is God but He does not demonstrate all the attributes of God while on the earth. Luke 2:52 blows out three of them. It says, "Jesus grew in wisdom and stature and favor with men and God." One of the attributes of God is that He is immutable. He cannot change. Luke says that He grew as in got taller and stronger. He changed. Next is that God is omniscient. He is all-knowing and therefore cannot learn anything new. This verse says that He grew in wisdom. Jesus learned new things as He grew older just like we do. He had to read and study and memorize Scripture just like all the other kids did during that time. Lastly, God is eternal so He cannot age but Jesus aged. This does not mean that Jesus ceased to be God but He was working out of His humanity during His time on earth. He did not demonstrate all the attributes of God. He was not all-present, all-knowing, or never changing. He was human.

Since He can relate to us then He is our example. Now we must know how Jesus was able to live a life like ours and still not sin. How was Jesus able to be tempted in every way we are and be betrayed and abandoned by everyone and still not sin? He did it by the Holy Spirit. This is where the Charismatics have wrong thinking. They put most of their emphasis on the Holy Spirit and not on Jesus. They center their thinking around the Holy Spirit being poured out on the day of Pentecost instead of the cross. The center of our faith should be Christ on the cross and not the Holy Spirit at Pentecost. Also there is no competition between the Holy Spirit and Jesus. Jesus lived as a man empowered by the Holy Spirit. That is how He was able to do all the great things that He did. The gospel of Luke proves this because it shows Jesus as the man and continually emphasizes the Holy Spirit's leading. In Luke 1 and 2 it says that an angel showed up and stated that Jesus would be born of the Virgin Mary. The angel said that she would conceive by the power of the Holy Spirit. The angel also said that He should be called Christ which means the one anointed with the Holy Spirit. This means that He would be fully empowered by the Holy Spirit. Then in Luke 3:16 John is baptizing people and He says, "I baptize you with water, but pretty soon Jesus will come and He will baptize you with the Holy Spirit." After this, when Jesus is baptized the Holy Spirit descends on Him in the image of a dove. God made the Holy Spirit visible so that everyone would know that Jesus would live His life by the power of the Holy Spirit. Next, in Luke 4 it says that He was full of the Holy Spirit and led by the Holy Spirit into the wilderness to be tempted. This means that to live like Jesus we must be Spirit-filled. Also when He was tempted, He refuted the devil with Scripture that He had memorized from Deuteronomy. After all of this, He starts His public ministry by going into the synagogue and reading Isaiah 61:1, which says, "The Spirit of the Lord is upon me." It continues throughout the book of Luke. It says many times that everything Jesus did was by the Holy Spirit. This gives great encouragement because if Jesus leaned into His divinity, then that is the only way to live this life. This means that we would have no hope because we have no divinity to lean into. Instead, Jesus leaned into the Holy Spirit and we are able to be empowered by the Holy Spirit like Jesus was. If you are a Christian and have given your life over to Jesus, then you have the Holy Spirit living and active inside you. You can lean on it to empower you throughout your whole life. This is how we live the kind of life Jesus lived. Also, with the Holy Spirit come the gifts of the Spirit. This is where Jesus healed and cast out demons and prophesied. We have the power within us to do all the great things Jesus did because we have the Holy Spirit.

Jesus is our example and can relate to us in every way. This means that when you are suffering or you do not know how to handle a particular situation, you can reach out and pray to Jesus for it. He will answer and the Spirit will give you exactly what you need to overcome whatever it is that you are going through. That is how Jesus lived. That is how we are supposed to live.

†

CHAPTER 10

Jesus Died to Cleanse Our Filth

In the last chapter I outlined how Jesus was able to live a sinless life through the power of the Holy Spirit. I hope you learned a lot from it and that you will be able to turn away from sin through the Holy Spirit. Now I want to discuss what Jesus has done for the sin that we have already committed and our future sins. In the beginning of this book I discussed how Jesus forgives us of our sin but I want to discuss what the sin does to us and our soul. I am going to talk about the doctrine of expiation. This is where God cleanses us from our sin. For you to understand this I am going to need to show you a lot of Scripture about what sin does to us.

The doctrine of expiation is how God cleanses our sin stained soul. This is a rarely addressed topic because

71

it is invisible. It is not like a stain on a shirt or a wound that is on our body. This is what sin does to our soul and we cannot see it so we really do not believe that we have anything to cure. Also, there are many people that believe it cannot be cured. To explain this I need to first talk about the doctrine of sin. There are two types of sin. The first is called a sin of omission, which is when something bad happens because of negligence. The second is called a sin of commission, which is when something that should not have happened has, because of bad actions. I will give you an example. There is a high school girl who has a father that does not really pay a lot of attention to what she does and he doesn't love her or protect her like he should. That is the sin of omission. Because of this she meets a guy that is dangerous and does drugs and alcohol and is just not a good guy. This guy has sex with her and does terrible things that should have never happened. This is the sin of commission. These two sins almost always work together. The most common way for a sin of commission to happen is when there is a sin of omission that has happened as well. Anytime either of these occur, we get touched and are stained by the sin that we have committed. This does not just happen by our sin. If someone sins against us and hurts us, we are also stained. For instance, if a woman was raped, she will be stained by that sin even though she was the victim. This is what sin is like. It pollutes everything that it touches no matter who commits it because there is that sin of omission. This is where it gets tricky. We know that when we commit a sin, we can go to Christ and He will take our sin away, but many of us don't know what to do when we are sinned against. We really can't ask forgiveness for things that were done to us. We can only ask forgiveness for the things that we have done. This puts us at a loss. We have no way to get rid of the stain on our soul. The truth is that we can be cleansed by Jesus' death.

To explain all of this we need to see how the Bible shows sin as being a stain on the soul. In Psalm 106:39 is says, "They defiled themselves by what they did." Proverbs 30:11-12 says, "There are those who curse their fathers and do not bless their mothers; those who are pure in their own eyes and are not cleansed from their filth. These two verses define it as defilement and filth. Mark 7:20 says, "It is not what goes into you but what comes out of your heart that makes you unclean." These all define that sin in some way makes us dirty and stained. Many people can feel this when they commit a sin. They say that they feel disgusting or dirty and they just want to take a shower. That is because they are actually feeling the defilement on their soul. It is not just physical, but spiritual. So what causes defilement? In Ezekiel 14:11 it talks about a day when people will no longer defile themselves by their sin, simply showing that all people are defiled by sin. Also you do not need to have something enormous or catastrophic happen to be defiled. It is any sin that you have ever committed and any sin that has ever been committed against you.

Another way that we become defiled is by a spiritual sin. Leviticus 19:31 says, "Do not turn to mediums or seek out spirits, for you will be defiled by them." Defilement comes through wrong spiritual practices. This does not just happen by you, yourself, mixing Christianity with other religions but can happen by others pushing their religion on you. For instance, when you were a child, your parents might have cast a spell over you and that would make you defiled. It stains your soul.

The third way defilement happens is how violence stains the soul. Lamentations 4:14 says that some people are defiled by blood. America is a very murderous country. If you don't believe it then just look at how many abortions take place here every day. Abortion is truly murder and it defiles everyone that is apart of it. Also people that were beat by their dad or women that are beat by their husbands are defiled because of it. This is because we were made in the likeness of God and when behavior like this happens it is diminishing and degrading. It defiles what we are supposed to be.

The fourth way defilement happens is probably the most pervasive and it is sexual sins. Sexual sin is a widespread epidemic all over the world. This is mainly because of the myth that what we do with our body does not affect our soul. It does. It stains our soul. In Genesis 34:5 Jacob hears that his daughter, Dinah, had been defiled. She was raped. That is what defiled her. She did not want it to happen but it happened and it stained her. Women are known as more likely to be raped but we need to know that men can be raped too. It is extremely rare for a man to admit that He has been raped because it is very degrading for him. It leaves a huge stain on the soul. Another way of soul-staining by sexual means is told in 1 Chronicles 5:1 saying that Reuben defiled his father's marriage bed. Reuben had sex with his stepmother. This is incest and it will not only ruin the relationship with whoever is involved with it forever but it will also stain the soul. A third of the people reading this book have been raped, molested, or abused sexually in some way. It happens and it stains the soul. Another example is in Numbers 5:27. This talks of a woman who defiled herself by being unfaithful to her husband. She was committing adultery and it defiled her. It will defile you and it will defile your marriage.

This happens even to people who are not married. If you are having any type of sexual contact with someone that you are not yet married to, then you are defiling yourself and your marriage in the future. One thing that many Christians do on this subject is only talk about how it affects the physical body. We threaten people with the possibility of contracting some sexually transmitted disease and we don't look at the fact that it stains and hurts the soul. It affects the person from the inside out. Lastly, in Leviticus 21:14 it says that a woman is defiled by prostitution. The definition of prostitution is the exchange of a sexual favor for compensation. This means that if you paid for pornography, you paid for prostitution. This also means that a strip club is prostitution because you gave money for seeing these women naked. This also means if you go on a date with a girl and buy her dinner and later on that evening have sex, it could be considered prostitution because you are receiving sex for buying her dinner. It is the exchange of anything sexual for something else and it defiles.

The last way that we can be defiled is by defilement. This is when we get defiled and then use it as an excuse to continue to defile ourselves. Hebrews 12:15 speaks of a bitter root that grows up to cause trouble and defile many. When we are sinned against and do not forgive, we get bitter. This bitterness then causes us to turn away from God. We can also become bitter toward God because He allowed something to happen to us. We become bitter at our parents, pastors, or coaches because they did not protect us through the sin of omission. The victim has a justifiable reason to be angry at the person that has wronged them, but if they harbor unforgiveness, they become bitter. This will result in us becoming defiled. When someone realizes this, they decide to keep hurting themselves and others.

Scripture also shows three aspects of defilement. The first is the defilement of place. In Leviticus 18:24-30 and Numbers 35:34 God speaks of locations that became defiled. This is like when it is very hard for you to go near a place where something bad happened to you. It is because that place is defiled. It is filthy and unclean. There are women that hate going into their bedroom because they have slept with other men and now their bedroom is defiled.

Things can also become defiled. Hebrews 13:4 says that the marriage bed should be kept pure and undefiled. The marriage bed can become defiled if the husband or wife has sex with someone else in it. When this happens it makes that bed defiled and when the other spouse finds out they absolutely hate that bed because it has been defiled. They will usually throw that bed out and get a new one because it is filthy and unclean to them.

Lastly, people can become defiled. In the Old Testament, there are many different ceremonial types of washing that all the people performed. When reading about these ceremonial washings, it looks like they all have some weird type of OCD. They are always going and bathing in the river and they always must do it in a certain way. This happens because God uses outward expressions to demonstrate what is happening inwardly. If you think about all of this, then you should see that Jesus broke all of the cultural taboos of His time. He was friends with adulterers and tax collectors that ripped people off. They were dirty and defiled and yet Jesus dwelt with them.

Now we are going to look at Genesis 3 and see the way this happened with the first sin. In Genesis 3 Adam and Eve were made in the likeness of God and they were both beautiful, glorious, and built for dignity. The Bible also says that they were both naked and were without shame. Shame was not even a concept at this time. Then they sinned against God and each other and immediately they felt shame. This happened because they were stained by their sin. The way they tried to deal with their shame was twofold. In relation to God they hid from Him. In relation to each other they covered themselves with fig leaves. The result is that sin leads to shame instead of repentance. Instead of going to God and asking forgiveness, they hid themselves because of the shame they felt. We do this all the time when we sin. We try to find a way to mask the shame or make it go away and there are three ways that we do this. The first one is trying to being the good person. We help everybody and memorize all these scriptures. This is the person that shows up early and stays late. They try to live as selflessly and sacrificially as they can. They do all this so that people will think they are completely fine, when instead they have all this shame inside. This is a way that they try to mask their shame to hide it from others.

The second option is to be the fun person. They are the life of the party. They can laugh about anything and it seems like nothing bothers them. They do this because they believe that no one wants to be with a sad and shameful person. They put on this mask that shows they are not hurt by anything and are always doing fine.

The third identity is just being tough. They are acting like they are impenetrable and that nothing can hurt them. As a result of all this people are compensating for their shame by toughness, or righteousness, or being the life of the party. Underneath all this they are ashamed. What this does is mess with our identity because our identity is mostly made up of our past. This means that we need to find the right way to cope with our past that doesn't allow us to get close to God and have us keep playing this role. This leaves us with three options on defining our identity.

One is that we can have our identity defined by what we have done. This is like saying you are an alcoholic so now for the rest of your life you are going to be an alcoholic. This happens with many people. Christian women that have slept with other guys in the past will believe that they can only marry someone who has slept with someone else too. You cannot allow your identity to be set by what you've done because Jesus died to make you a new creation.

The second option is to let your identity be defined by what people have done to you. An example of this is when a woman is raped. Because of this she decides that she is now dirty and because she is dirty, she is going to do dirty things. She will believe that she must have sex with many men because that is what a dirty person does. This is one reason why women become prostitutes. They were raped and then believe that that is all they can do.

The third and final option is the only hope and is the only way to be cleansed from your defilement and shame. It is to let your identity be shaped by what Jesus has done for you. I will explain this by looking at the Old Testament section on atonement. Leviticus

16:30 says, "This day of atonement will be made for you, to cleanse you. Then, before the Lord, you will be clean from all your sin." The Day of Atonement was to cleanse the Israelites from all their sin. Jesus made atonement for us on the cross. If we surrender and submit our lives to Jesus, then He will make atonement for us through His death and we are able to be cleansed from all our sin. We are the bride of Christ. Brides always wear white as a symbol that they are pure. That tradition comes from the Bible. We are to be pure and without stain. The only way to be cleansed from the stains that we have because of sin is through the death and resurrection of Jesus Christ. He went to the cross to cleanse all the filth from our lives forever.

CHAPTER 11

Jesus Died to Reveal God

In this book I have covered many things but have left out one large part. Mostly this book is about Jesus so it makes sense that there is a great emphasis on Him. I also did a chapter devoted to how the Holy Spirit can work in our life. The person I kind of left out is God. I mentioned Him many times and talked about Him a lot, but I did not take as much time as I should have to show Him in light of the cross. Well, now is the time to do that.

The number one question that is always asked when dealing with the issue of God is, "How do I get to know God?" Everyone wants to be able to know God and there are many views of how to do that. The atheists say that there is no God so He obviously can't be known. Others say that there is a God but He does not allow Himself to be known. Then some people say that God dwells in you and you have a spark of the divine in you somewhere. This means that you need to turn inward and meditate and get to know yourself and then you will know God. Then still others say that it is an external quest and that you need to go visit some holy place and there you will get a revelation of God. And finally others would say that you can get in touch with God through creation and nature because He is the Creator of everything. Now most of these reasons have some truth to them except for the fact that these cannot help you to know God. There is truly only one way to even try to understand who He is, and that way is by looking at Jesus Christ. We must always go to Jesus. You want to know God then you have got to go to Jesus. In John 1:18 it says, "No one has ever seen God, but God the one and only who is at the Father's right side has made Him known." The Christians have a concept that I mentioned earlier about God that is different than all other religions. We believe in the Trinity, which are three persons in one. We have the Father, the Son, and the Holy Spirit all in one that is God. The Son is the one that sits at the Father's right side and is just as much God as the other two. This also shows why people are relational. The Bible says that we were made in the likeness of Him and God is always in a relationship with the rest of the Trinity, so we were made to be in relationships too. What John was overall saying is that the first part of God, the Father, is spirit and is invisible. No one can see Him. There is the Son, though, that has seen Him and He became a human being. That is why Christmas is celebrated. It is not about getting a bunch of presents. Christmas is about celebrating the greatest gift that was ever given. It was the Gift of gifts. It was Jesus Christ. God was born into human history and lived just like we do. Because of this we can see and learn and hear from and testify about who God is because Jesus was making Him known. In John 14:8-9 Jesus had a conversation with a man named Philip. Phillip said, "Show us the Father and that would be good enough for us." All He wanted was to see God and was asking God to show Him to him. He did not realize who Jesus truly was but Jesus corrected him by answering, "Don't you know me, Phillip, even after I have been among you for such a long time? Anyone who has seen me has seen the Father." Right there Jesus told everyone that He is one and the same as the Father. He is God. Philip is asking to see God and Jesus just says, "I have been hanging out with you all day. What more do you want?" You want to be able to see God, look to Jesus. Paul says in Colossians 1:15 that Jesus is the image of the invisible

God. Now we need to address what part of Jesus' life that we need to look at so we can know God. Some would say that we should look at His great teachings. Others would say look at His works. Still others would say to look at His miracles. These are all great and good things that Jesus did but the Bible seems to focus on the cross more than anything else in Jesus' life. This is the place we need to go to know God.

We learn about God's attributes, character, essence, and nature more than any other place in the Bible at Jesus' crucifixion. This is where you can find everything you need to know. This is the act that the entire Bible and this book stand on. It is the greatest act in the history of the world. It is the death of the Savior. There are many different aspects that we can examine by looking at Jesus' death but we will examine six very important ones.

The first aspect of God we see is His justice. This is the one attribute that people are least fond of. I guess it must be because we are sinners. The truth is that justice is a great and beautiful thing. God desires all people to be treated with equality and dignity through the rule of law. This is why God is a just God. This means that when God sees sin, He has to deal with it. If He overlooks it, then He would deny His own justice. Well, we are sinners and are unjust and therefore can't be with God because He is perfectly just. This causes a great gap in our relationship with Him but there is hope. In Romans 3:25-26 it says, "God presented Him as a sacrifice of atonement through faith in His blood. He did this to demonstrate His justice because in His forbearance He had left the sins committed beforehand unpunished." God offered His Son, Jesus, up to be the sacrifice that was needed because of our sins. That is the only way that we could have been acquitted from the penalty of our sins, which is death. He did this to be just by punishing the sins that we have committed. This shows us the great and perfect justice of God.

We also see the second point, which is the love of God. It was an act of love that God sent Jesus to die instead of sending me to die. The Bible says that God loves us like a Father. This is hard for some people because they grow up with a bad father or no father at all. Some of my close friends have grown up in very abusive homes where their dad left when they were very young and they had to become the man in the family. My heart breaks for these people because they end up having no idea what a true man is to be. All these guys know is a father that is truly just a boy. In our society we have made becoming a man a certain age or a certain action. We say that a guy is a man when he turns twenty-one and can drink or when He has sex for the first time or does an unbelievable task. This has blurred the line that shows us when we cross into manhood so much that we can never know when we are men or when we are still boys. Because of this we have many boys running around the world and are running dangerously short on men. The Bible says that God is a good Father. This means that anything that was not good or right about your earthly father is perfect in God. This also means that God is a true man. Jesus shows us what God is like so when we look at Jesus we can see who a true man is. Romans 5:8 says, "God demonstrates His love for us in this: while we were yet sinners, Christ died for us." If you ever wonder if God loves you or cares for you; you can look at the cross and see the perfect love of God. That is what a good father does. He tells us that He loves us and then shows us that He loves us. 1 John 3:16 says that the cross is how we know what love is. God revealed to us what love truly is in His son's death. We need to define love by what God has done for us. 1 John 4:9-10 says, "This is how God showed His love among us. He sent His one and only Son into the world that we might live through Him. This is love: not that we loved God, but that God loved us and sent His son as an atoning sacrifice for our sins." Our loving relationship with God does not start with us loving Him, but with Him loving us from the very beginning. God came on a rescue mission to find us and save us from eternal death. He was on a mission of love to come and rescue us.

In the person of Jesus Christ we see that God is just by punishing sin and sinners. Then we see the love of God by sending His son to take away our sins. The result of this is that we are given reconciliation with God. This is the relational aspect of God's heart toward us. Sin has a separating effect. What happens is we join together with people and sin tears us apart from them and even God. Sin has a repelling and separating effect that causes people to not come close or want to be around us. It ruins our friendships, our marriages, relationship with our parents, and even our relationship with other Christians. One of the themes in the book of Isaiah is that our sin has separated us from God. What we need is reconciliation. We need some way that our sin can be taken away so we can have an intimate relationship that we long for with God. This was accomplished on the cross. We see the justice of God punishing sin and the love of God saving us from being killed and by this we are reconciled back to God. This is explained in Romans 5:10-11, which says, "For if, when we were God's enemies, we were reconciled to Him through the death of His Son, how much more, having been reconciled shall we be saved through His life? Not only is this so, but we also rejoice in God through our Lord Jesus Christ, through whom we have now received reconciliation." Jesus takes away our sin through His death and now we have a reconciled relationship with God. There are probably some of you reading this book that know they have not prayed nor had a true relationship with God for many years if ever, and are wondering if they can still be reconciled. The answer is always yes. It does not matter what you have done, you can always come back into the loving arms of God through Jesus. In justice He must deal with sin, and in love He has dealt with sin through Jesus. It is by Jesus that reconciliation has been made so we can have a relationship with God. Paul talks about this in 2 Corinthians 5:18-21 when He says, "All of this is from God, who reconciled us to Himself through Christ and gave us the ministry of reconciliation." The ministry of reconciliation is one of the great privileges of being a Christian. It means that when we sin against someone, we can go to them and ask forgiveness and can be forgiven and not have that sin held against us. This gives us a reconciled friendship with that person. This has very practical implications because we know that when sin comes between people we want blood. If we let sin into our relationships, before long we really just want to kill the person. You don't want to acknowledge yourself as doing this but you know it is true. I have had people that are close to me that have wronged me and at times I wished they would just go and die. This is why reconciliation is so important. It gives us the love we had for that person back so we can have a relationship that is not harmed by sin anymore.

This all pleases God. When Jesus went to the cross, God was not executing His plan out of fear or necessity. He was doing it out of His love and pleasure, which is the fourth point. Isaiah 53:10 says that it was the Lord's will to crush Him and cause Him to suffer. God was pleased to secure our salvation through the work of His Son.

He did that through His wisdom and power which is my fifth point. Because God is wise, He knows how to deal with the human condition of sin. Him being powerful means that He not only knows what to do, but is able to do it. These must go hand in hand otherwise there would be no way that God could save us from our sin. He would either know what to do but not be able to do it, or not know what to do, yet be able to do it. He must be both. In 1 Corinthians 1:17 Paul says, "For Christ did not send me to baptize, but to preach the Gospel, not with words of human wisdom, lest the cross be emptied of its power." Paul is actually saying right here that he is not a good preacher. He could write great letters but when He shows up you're expecting to see Dwayne Johnson and you get Woody Allen. He was one of the most unimpressive people of that time. What Paul is getting at is that people do not follow Jesus because He is well-marketed. It is that the power of Jesus is so real and true that it changes the hearts and lives of people. God succeeds despite the preaching or marketing of Christianity. Christianity doesn't succeed through the hipness, coolness, and trendiness, but through the power of Jesus to change lives. Paul goes on to say that the message of the cross is foolishness to those that are perishing. It actually sounds pretty crazy to people that are not Christians. To them, when we explain our faith, what they hear is that there was and is an eternal God that spoke everything into existence. Then we sinned against Him because we ate fruit while we were naked because a snake told us to. Then thousands of years later a virgin gave birth to a baby. He was born in a feeding trough. He never committed a sin and then died on a cross for you. Looking at it this way it sounds completely crazy, yet this is what we believe. The problem is that many people try to make it less crazy and unbelievable to where they don't have the truth and then there is no power. It is only by the power of Jesus that people believe. Anyone that believes Christianity for any other reason does not believe the truth. This is a great apologetic point though. There is no way that anyone could make this up. You could say that it is a story so unbelievable that it must be true. It is only by the power and wisdom of God that we are saved. Soren Kierkagaard was a great Danish philosopher, who gave a parable that explains this very clearly. He said that there was once a very mighty king and that he was very rich and strong and wise. All the women in the kingdom wanted to marry him because of his money and power. The king did not want to marry any of these women because he knew that they would only marry him for the benefits that they would earn. It would not be because of love. Then one day he saw a woman that was born to a peasant family working in the fields. He wanted to get to know her so he put on peasant's clothes and assigned himself as a simple common laborer in the vineyard next to her. He worked next to her every day and never let her know that he was the king. He fell in love with her because he got to know her and she fell in love with him because she got to know him. Eventually he proposed and she accepted because she truly wanted to marry him. Then on her wedding day, the man came dressed as the king. She thought that she would live a life of simplicity and poverty, but instead she was given the benefits of the kingdom. This is what Jesus did. He came as a peasant and lived among us and got to know us. He lived like us and worked like us and died like us. If we love Him like His bride, then He shares with us the benefits of the kingdom. We see the power of God to identify with us in the person of Jesus and take away our sin so that the justice of God could be met, so that the love of God could be given, so that the reconciliation with God could be made possible, that the pleasure of God in relationship could be actualized through the wisdom and power of God through the person and the work of Jesus on the cross.

The culmination of this all is my sixth and final point. This is all for the glory of God. When you look at the person of Jesus, you see a life fully devoted and submitted to nothing else but the glory of God. We were ultimately made to glorify God. Lucifer, which is Satan, was an archangel, which means He is one of the head angels, who was made to lead praises and glorify God. When Lucifer fell from heaven, one-third of the angels went with him and they were most likely the angels that were under him so there were no angels to glorify God. Then we were created to love and bring glory to God but because of our sin we were led astray from God. To fix this, God sent His only Son to come and die for us and reveal Him to us so that those who love Him may give Him glory forever. That is what the cross is all about. It is us coming back to God and giving

Him glory for what He has done. If you want to live a happy life, I can tell you that you cannot be happier than doing what you were specifically created for and that is to glorify God.

CHAPTER 12

Who Jesus Died For

So far in this book we have covered Jesus taking away our sin, Jesus taking our wrath, Jesus crushing our enemies, Jesus giving us His righteousness, Jesus as our example, and a few other subjects that all were accomplished when Jesus died on the cross. In this chapter we are going to go very deep into theology so I hope you're ready. While going through this it is amazing what Jesus has done but truly none of these things matter at all unless we know exactly who Christ died for? If we do not know the answer to that question, then Jesus' death doesn't mean a thing to us. So we are going to look at the five main views that try to answer this question. Two are wrong, two are alright, and the fifth one is the one that I believe and I hope that you will also.

The first view is Universalism. This belief says that everyone goes to heaven. Universalists teach that people are not actually sinners but just basically good moral people. This is proven completely wrong though Scripture. Psalm 51:5 says, "We're sinners from our mother's womb." Psalm 58:3 says, "We go astray from our mother's womb." Some people say that the book of Psalms is not truly literal. Fine then I'll give you Romans 3:23. "All have sinned and fall short of the glory of God." This undeniably proves that we are sinners. Universalists also say that they don't believe in hell. This is wrong because in Matthew 10:28 Jesus says, "Do not be afraid of those that can kill the body but cannot kill the soul. Rather, be afraid of the one that can destroy both body and soul in hell." Obviously this view is wrong. They will also say that Jesus died to save nobody. This view gives no true answer to who Jesus died for.

The second view is a modified version of this that is called Pelagianism. This belief is named after a monk named Pelagius who taught that all people are good and will go to heaven. The only difference between Universalism and Pelagianism is that Pelagians believe that there is a hell, but is only for the devil and his angels. This fails on the same points that Universalism does and also says that Jesus died to save no one.

Now we are going to look at the beliefs that I considered to be alright. By saying that they are alright, I mean that you can fully believe one of them if you want and still be fine. Personally, though, I do not completely believe either of them. The next two views are Calvinism and Arminianism. These views have been debated over more than anything else within the church. This is one of the debates that has actually split the church in two. Well I plan to clear that up right now. Arminianism comes from a man named James Arminius, who was a student under John Calvin, which is the person from which Calvinism comes from. Arminius said that he does not agree with everything that Calvin believes but that the commentaries on the Bible that he gave are great. When Arminius had followers they created the five points of Arminianism. After this happened the Calvinists looked at the five points of Arminianism and then created the five points of Calvinism by writing the exact opposite of what the Arminians did. I am going to go through all five points of both views at the same time and will show which ones I find to be true and the reasons why. The first point of Arminianism is Free Will. Truly, there is no such thing as Free Will. The reason is that I can Will myself to never die and I will still die. I can Will myself to be ten feet tall and will still be the same height that I am. We are not free to have whatever we Will happen. There is however free choice. God gives us many choices in this life and one of those choices is that we can decide to follow Him or not. The first point of Calvinism is total depravity. This means that everything that we choose to do is evil or has a bad motive behind it. For example, a guy might choose to help a girl move to another place, which is a good thing to do. Although, his motive is that by doing this she might sleep with him. That is an evil motive. I do believe this one. One thing you must understand though is that total depravity does not mean utter depravity. Utter depravity means that we can never do anything good ever. Total depravity means that on our own we cannot do anything good. For us to be able to do good we must have God and His Spirit. This is what makes us able to choose God. The Bible says that we can never know God unless the Spirit opens up our heart to Him. The Spirit must open up our heart and then we have a chance to choose to follow Him. So I believe both of these to a degree.

The second point of Arminianism is conditional election. This means that God can only choose to save people that choose Him back. I agree with this one. The second point of Calvinism is unconditional election. This means that no matter if they choose God or not, God can still choose them to be saved. I also believe this one to a degree. I believe this because if it is not true then there would be no way for aborted babies to go to heaven. Or newborns that die to go to heaven. A person that does not have the capacity in his mind to choose God doesn't have any hope if this if not true. So I believe both of these points to a degree.

The third point of Arminianism is unlimited atonement and the third point of Calvinism is limited atonement. I am going to skip these because they are actually the main topics of the next viewpoint.

The fourth point of Arminianism is resistible grace, which means that God can show you His grace and you can turn away from it. The fourth point of Calvinism is irresistible grace and means that if God shows His grace to you, then there is no way you can turn away from it. I believe resistible grace because of the one unforgivable sin. The unforgivable sin is given in Mark 3:28-29 which says, "I promise you that any of the sinful things that you say or do can be forgiven, no matter how terrible those things are. But if you blaspheme the Holy Spirit, you can never be forgiven." To blaspheme the Holy Spirit means that the Spirit opens up to you and you choose to deny the Spirit and turn away from God. This means that we can resist the grace of God.

The fifth point of Arminianism is perseverance of some saints which means that a person that is saved can later choose to turn their back on God. The fifth point of Calvinism is perseverance of all saints which means that everyone who has ever been saved will remain saved until they die and go to heaven. I believe in the perseverance of all saints because a saint is someone who is truly saved. If someone is truly saved, then they cannot turn away from God because they have surrendered their entire life to Him. People who say they were saved and are not anymore were actually never truly saved in the first place. This is basically the debate of once saved always saved and if you were truly saved then you can never turn your back on God. Now you should be confused because I believe parts of both of them. Arminianism says that Jesus died for everyone in the world and to be saved we must choose Him. Calvinism says that Jesus died for those that God has picked to be saved and no one else. These are both very different, so how can they both in some way be right? Before I go into that I do want you to be aware of one thing. Both of these beliefs are Christian. This is an in-house debate. This should not be something that divides us as the church, especially when there is truth in both of them. We can discuss this all we want but in the end, we should not let it divide us like it has for such a long time. Is there any Scripture that proves either of these beliefs? The Arminianist will begin with Isaiah

53:6 which says, "Each person has turned his own way, and the Lord has laid on Him the iniquity of us all." See it says that Jesus died for all. Then there is 1 Timothy 2:3-6 which says, "God our savior, who wants all men to be saved and come to the knowledge of the truth, for there is one God, one mediator between God and man, the man Jesus Christ Who gave Himself as a ransom for all men." This says that Christ gave Himself for all men. John 1:29 says, "Behold the Lamb of God who takes away the sins of the world." Not some, the entire world. Finally they will end with John 3:16 which says, "For God so loved the world that He gave His only Son that whosoever believes in Him will not perish but have everlasting life." This verse says the world and whosoever. So now we have a pile of Arminian verses. The Calvinist will then step up and will just start to argue over the points and then will say that when the verses say all, it really means some. There are many different languages and different ways to translate the Bible from its original language, but when it said all, it meant all. Then they will also say that when it says the world it means the different nations and tongues, which is the definition the Bible does use a few times, but in these verses it means everyone in the world. The Aminianist will then ask for some verses and the Calvinist is happy to pull out Matthew 1:21 which says,

"At His birth, it was promised that Jesus will save His people from their sins." Not all, just His people. Then there is Matthew 20:28 that says, "Jesus did not come to be served, but to serve and give His life as a ransom for many." Not all, just many. The last one is John 10:11 where Jesus says, "I am the good shepherd. The good shepherd lays down his life for the sheep." See, not the goats or cows just the sheep. Now we have one pile of Arminian verses and one pile of Calvinist verses so which one is right? They both have verses to back them up and there is truth in both of them so how can one be wrong? Well the answer is that they are both right to a degree.

The fifth view is the one that I believe and it combines Calvinism and Arminianism together. It is called Unlimited Limited Atonement. Some people will say that this is actually what John Calvin believes. In John Calvin's commentary on Galatians 5:12 he said, "It is God's will that we should seek the salvation of all men, as Christ suffered for the sins of the whole world." Right here he sounds a lot like an Arminian and says that Calvinism is not true. Do you see what I am doing? I am defeating Calvinism with Calvin. Now that is talent. Calvinism came about after Calvin died, and the first generation of Calvinists were good. The second generation got a little iffy. The third generation got a little iffier and now they are way off. This is how Arminian and Calvinism are reconciled. It is in the belief of Unlimited Limited Atonement. I will use one verse and an illustration to prove this view. The verse I will use is 1 Timothy 4:10 and it says, "We have put our hope in the living God, who is the savior of all men, especially those who are saved." How can Jesus be the savior of all men and those who are saved? This is possible because of the spread of Christianity. Anywhere Christianity has spread there are morals that people follow and we actually do the right things most of the time. Anywhere that Christianity has not spread, they are eating their neighbor for dinner. Jesus died so that we could have morals and be able to follow them. In that way, He has saved all people. He also died for those who are saved and they are especially saved because when they die they get to go and be with Jesus in heaven. This is what Unlimited Limited Atonement means; that God saved all men by letting us live in this world with morals and especially saved those that choose God because they get to go to heaven. The illustration I will use is the Day of Atonement. The Jews call this Yom Kipper. On this day, when they had the tabernacle, the priest would give a sacrifice that was to cover the sins of the whole nation of Israel. This is the unlimited part. All of Israel was blessed because they were able to still live in that nation. The people that loved God would bring their own sacrifice and name their sin and then sacrifice it. By doing this, they were completely washed clean. This is the limited part. They were the ones that would actually be given the chance when Jesus died for everyone's sin. The others would actually go to hell because they didn't truly love God but were blessed because they lived in the nation of Israel. These days, to be saved we confess our sins to God, repent, and surrender our lives to His will and then we are saved and are able to go to heaven. This is how it was at the beginning of the Bible and is how it has always been. The atonement is unlimited and yet limited at the same time.

✠

CHAPTER 13

The Final Achievement

We have reached the end of this journey of studying every achievement made by Jesus dying on the cross, but there is one more that I want to look at. Isaiah 53:5 says, "He was pierced for our transgressions, He was crushed for our iniquity." Our transgressions are the sins that we commit. Our iniquity in this tense is translated to mean our inward turn toward evil. Iniquity is the part inside of every human that desires evil. If we look at Adolf Hitler, we see a man that killed hundreds of thousands of Jews. He did great and terrible evil. There is also Joseph Stalin who killed hundreds of his own people. There are sex traffickers that sell thirteen year old girls to men every night. There are child molesters, murderers, thieves, and liars. Some of these people did not fully believe that what they did was evil. Hitler and Stalin did not believe that what they were doing was wrong. What if they were shown the depth of their evil? What if at one time they saw exactly how terrible it was and the enormity of their sin that they had committed? At that time they would cry out, "My God, My God why have you forsaken me?' They did not cry that out though. Jesus cried that out on the cross. He took theirs and our iniquity upon Himself. When He did that He was actually separated from God. Jesus separated Himself from God so that we would never have to be. That is the beauty of the cross. I want to end with this thought in your mind. You are the reason Jesus died. If you were the only one that would be saved by His death, He would have still done it. It was for you that He had the nails driven into His wrists and legs. It was for you that He was pierced in the side. It was all for you and because of that, it is as if you were the one that crucified Him. You are the one that put Him on the cross and He still loves you. I will end this book with a lyric from the band Sidewalk Prophets. This lyric made me cry the first time I heard it and it still will make me cry when I see the depth of God's love more than anything else.

"I am the man who cried out from the crowd for your
    blood to be spilled on this earth shaking ground.

I turned away with a smile on my face with this
sin in my heart trying to bury your grace.
Alone in the night I still call out to you so
ashamed of my life, my life, my life.
But you love me anyway."

Quotes and information

Josephus

C.S. Lewis

Joseph Smith

Mohammed

Soren Kierkagaard

James Arminius

John Calvin

Sidewalk Prophets

Mark Driscoll

Matt Carter

Ron Luce

Verses: